A Heart Full of Thanks

ISBN: 978-93-6081-939-2
Price:499.00
Publishing Year 2024

Published by: **Perfect Writer**
Head Office: X-159/1 Street no. 11 Brahmpuri, Near Brahmpuri Public School New Delhi 110053
Phones: +91 8982099954
Email: publish@perfectwriter.in
Website: www.perfectwriter.in

A Heart Full of Thanks

Shivam Singh Bhadauriya

Acknowledgement

I want to say a big thank you to some amazing people who have been a huge part of making this book happen. First, I'm really thankful to Ruksana. She's been there with me, guiding me and giving me the push to dream big.

A big shoutout to Vipin. He's been there, guiding me and supporting me all the way.

I also want to thank Rhonda Byrne, the author of "The Secret." Her words have made me see how powerful gratitude can be.

Thanks to Varun as well. He helped me a lot with the research and writing of this book.

I can't forget to thank all the sources and technology that made writing this book possible.

And a special thanks to my family and friends. Your support and belief in what I wanted to do have been incredible.
Lastly, a big thank you to the publisher. This book is here because of their belief in it.

To everyone I've mentioned, your help and support mean the world to me. This book is a result of all of you being a part of my journey.

Contents

Why This Book? vii

Introduction ix

Deeply understanding the importance of gratitude and appreciation xii

The Science behind Gratitude and appreciation xiv

Lesson 1: Art of Happiness 0

Difference between happiness and Joy 1

How to Find Happiness 2

Snapshot of Happiness 3

Lesson.2: Embracing Self-Love and Gratitude 5

Step-by-Step Guide About How to Love Yourself Unconditionally: 7

Lesson. 3: Gratitude and Belief 10

The Art of Manifesting Through Beliefs 12

Beliefs in Action 12

How to Change Your Self-Limiting Beliefs? 13

Lesson.4: The Foundation of a strong relationship 14

Relationship Challenge 15

Appreciation in Action: How Gratitude Transformed My Relationship 16

How to make any relationship strong 18

Lesson. 5: Finding Joy in Nature 21

Lesson 6: Gratitude for a better physical & mental health .. 24

Mindful Eating 24
What is Mindful Eating? 25
My Journey Towards Mindful Eating 26
Make your water work for you 28
Why Water Affirmation? 29
Lesson. 7: Ways through which you can practice gratitude 31
Blessings Book 33
A Jar full of goodness 37
Gratitude Guide: Your Daily Calendar of Positivity 40
Gratitude Mantras: Simple Words to Change Your Life 43
Meditation of Thanks 47
Lesson 8 Manifest your desires through Gratitude 52
Lesson 9: Heartfelt Appreciation 53
Lesson 10: Writing a Gratitude letter to the Universe 57

Why This Book?

Life is just a series of problems, one after another.
If you ever felt like this at any point of your life, this book is for you.

Maybe you've never read a single book in your life, or you started reading a typical self-help book, found it boring, and never completed it. This book is different; I guarantee it will keep you engaged from start to finish because of the impact of every single word in your life.

There are two types of people who will read this book. The first type includes those facing many challenges in life—struggling with money, missing out on opportunities, failing in business, or feeling unhappy. The second type includes those who are working to improve themselves and achieve their goals. For both types of people, this book is going to be a game-changer.

While reading this book, you will discover a life-changing secret. A secret that can turn your problems into blessings, your challenges into opportunities, your failures into successes, and your unhappiness into joy. This secret connects you to something bigger than yourself—whether you call it God, the Universe, Higher Consciousness, or whatever feels right to you.

This secret has been with us for ages, hidden within the teachings of ancient wisdom found in texts like the Vedas, Upanishads, Bhagavad Gita, Quran, Bible, and even the guidance of figures like Buddha, Krishna, Jesus, and Muhammad.

Imagine waking up each day, feeling genuinely happy, joyful and living a life you love, That's the promise that lies within these pages. It's like a treasure map to a life filled with contentment, love, and boundless happiness. But here's the thing: while this power can do more than you expected, most of us aren't fully aware of its true potential.

This book is your guide to unveiling this hidden power within you. It's not just about reading words; it's about starting a journey. A journey that takes you from the shadows of negativity, complaints, and difficulties to the realm of positivity, love, and bliss. It's a journey that ancient civilizations understood well, and now it's your turn.

Introduction

Why we are here on Earth and what our purpose in life is? Some people believe life has no specific purpose, that it's meaningless. Others think life's purpose is simply to work and eventually die. Some believe the purpose of life is to discover the purpose.

But what if I tell you that there is a simpler and more satisfying answer? What if I tell you that the purpose of life is to find joy, happiness, and entertainment in everything around you, travel, eat, dream, achieve and do everything we wish, easily and effortlessly.? Sounds too good to be true, right? It's actually backed by science, experience, and common sense.

Let me ask you something. Do you remember what it was like when you were in your mother's womb? Probably not, but let me tell you. It was amazing. Your body was preparing for life even before you were born. You were connected to your mother for nourishment. You had everything you needed to grow and thrive.

And then you came into this world. And guess what? You still had everything you needed to live and enjoy. You didn't have to worry about things like air, water, or your organs – they were all provided for you. You could walk with your own feet, see with your eyes, hear with your ears, and have all the essential organs within you.

How awesome is that? Think about it. Imagine if you had to do all these things on our own – life would be incredibly tough. But the Creator has made them freely available to you. But why? Here is a simple answer: He wants you to simply focus on finding joy, happiness, and entertainment in everything around you. He wants you to have fun, to explore, to learn, to play and to experience everything we want or wanted to experience before we came into this physical world.

And that's exactly what you did when you were a baby. Whether it was taking your first steps, speaking your first words, or playing with toys, you found delight in these experiences. You were curious, adventurous, and joyful.

But why did your natural instincts fade? Why did you start noticing problems? Well, it's because you were exposed to a lot of negative influences and distractions in the world. You were taught to compare yourself to others, to chase after just material things, to worry about the future, to regret the past, and to forget the present. You were bombarded with messages that told you that you were not good enough, not smart enough, not rich enough, not happy enough. You were conditioned to believe that joy and happiness were something outside of you, something that you had to earn, deserve, or find.

But that's not true. Love, Joy and happiness are not something outside of you, they are something inside of you. They are your natural state of being, your birthright, your gift from the Creator. You don't have to earn them, deserve them, or find them. You just have to remember them, rediscover them, and reclaim them.

How do you do that? The answer lies in these powerful concepts: gratitude and appreciation. This book will challenge and expand your understanding of them, revealing their profound impact on various aspects of life. It's not just about saying 'thank you'—it's a transformative practice that can achieve everything you desire. It can enhance your well-being, deepen your relationships, and bring a new level of joy and satisfaction to your daily experiences.

As you turn the pages, you'll be introduced to innovative ways to integrate gratitude and appreciation into your life, from the simplicity of mindful appreciation to the profound effects of a heartfelt 'thank you.' This isn't just another self-help book; it's a journey that will redefine your perspective on gratitude and its ability to reshape your reality.

You'll learn how gratitude and appreciation can be the keys to a more fulfilling life, one where challenges become opportunities for growth, and you can achieve everything you want. The lessons within these chapters are more than concepts; they are practical tools that will guide you towards a life flourishing with positivity and purpose.

Prepare yourself for an adventure that will enlighten, inspire, and empower you to live your dream life, grounded in the power of gratitude and appreciation.

Deeply understanding the importance of gratitude and appreciation

Gratitude and appreciation turn what little you have into abundance.

Religious traditions including Judaism, Christianity, Islam, Buddhism, and Hinduism all encourage cultivating gratitude as an part of our existence. Gratitude was also significant in ancient philosophies and cultures. In Roman culture, Cicero mentioned gratitude as the 'mother' of all human feelings.

The beginning of the Ramayana hints at the importance of gratitude. Among the 16 qualities that Valmiki envisioned for the person of perfection, one is to be a personification of gratitude, to possess gratefulness. Valmiki desired that this person should never be ungrateful; this is what he wanted his role important model to personify, to imbibe. Valmiki asked Narada, "Hey Narada Maharshi, who in the present world possesses all sixteen qualities?"

To this question, Narada replies that it is indeed Shree Raama of Ayodhya who has all these sixteen auspicious attributes, and specifically mentions that indeed he possesses this great quality of gratefulness or gratitude called 'kṛtajñatā'.

In Buddhism, gratitude holds profound significance, as it aligns with the core teachings and philosophies of Gautam Buddha. The Buddha said: "These two people are hard to find in the world. Which two? The one who is first to do a kindness, and the one who is grateful and thankful for a kindness done." Anguttara Nikaya (AN 2:118). Jeff Wilson (Shin Buddhist priest, author, and professor) says, "We don't practice Buddhism to achieve anything—not enlightenment, good karma, a favourable rebirth, or material rewards. We practice simply to give thanks for what we have received."

Gratitude and appreciation are the most powerful forms of worship in every religion because they spiritually connect us to the highest energy, which some call the Universe, God, or any other name you prefer. This highest energy can provide you with whatever you desire: love, happiness, your dream job, good health, and more. In Matthew 13:12, Jesus says, "Whoever has will be given more, and he will have an abundance. Whoever does not have, even what he has will be taken from him." This scripture from the Bible perfectly illustrates what gratitude can do for our lives. If you have gratitude, you will be given more reasons to be grateful; however, if you lack gratitude and are unappreciative, then even the good things you have will be taken away. Similarly, in the Quran, Surah Ibrahim (14:7) Allah says: "And remember, your Lord declared: If you are grateful, I will add more favours to you, but if you show ingratitude, truly My punishment is terrible."

The Science behind Gratitude and appreciation

"Gratitude is like a magnet; the more grateful you are, the more you will receive to be grateful for."

Albert Einstein said, "Everything is energy and that's all there is to it." He was referring to the Law of Vibration. This law states that everything in our universe, whether visible or not, is composed of pure energy or light when broken down to its simplest form. This energy vibrates and exists as a frequency or pattern. All people, things, and experiences have frequencies, and they are attracted to us based on the frequency of our thoughts. This means that to manifest something, we must first match the frequency of what we desire. The larger the desire, the higher the frequency required to attract it.

But how do we know at what frequency we are vibrating? Simply by assessing how we feel at any given moment, we can easily check our vibration. For example, if we feel excited, loving, or grateful, we are vibrating at a higher frequency. Whenever we appreciate people and things around us, our vibration is higher. When we are happy, our vibration is high. And the most special thing is that gratitude and appreciation hold the highest frequency in the universe, while hate, criticism, shame, anger, and jealousy possess the lowest frequency. If we maintain a constant state of gratefulness and appreciation, we continuously attract great things in life: good health, wealth, success, dream job, and more—whatever we desire. This is the great secret you've been unaware of until now. Most successful people this world has ever seen, knowingly or unknowingly, have been using the power of gratitude to achieve good things in life.

But what I mean when we say "gratitude" and "appreciation.”? Let’s figure out.

Gratitude is “the quality of being thankful; readiness to show appreciation for and to return kindness.” Appreciation, on the other hand, is “recognition and enjoyment of the good qualities of someone or something.” So, gratitude is like the general state of being, while appreciation is how we express that gratitude through our thoughts, attitudes, and actions. Gratitude sets the stage for appreciation to grow.

There are three types of gratitude: a "gratitude personality" (someone who generally tends to be grateful), a gratitude "mood" (how grateful you feel each day), and a gratitude "feeling" (a temporary feeling of gratitude you might have after someone gives you a gift or helps you). To explain it better, you can feel grateful for someone or something at a particular moment, and you can also develop gratitude as a long-term positive trait. This book aims to help you develop a lasting way of being grateful.

Lesson 1: Art of Happiness

"For every minute you are angry you lose sixty seconds of happiness." — Ralph Waldo Emerson

We're not here just to make money, yeah, money is important to survive and thrive in this world but it is not the only thing we're here for. We're here to be happy and to do things that make us happy for a long time. Long ago, people didn't even use money. According to Sadhguru (Spiritual guru and yogi, founder of Isha yoga centre) "Happiness is our nature. If we go against our own nature to be happy, we will never get anywhere. To be happy is not the ultimate aspect of life. It is the fundamental aspect of life. If you are not happy, what else can you do with your life? Only if you are happy, can other great possibilities arise in your life."

In this lesson, we'll see how gratitude and appreciation can lead to enduring happiness and joy. But before we get into that, we need to understand the difference between happiness and joy. We often use these words like they mean the same thing, but they're actually different. We'll learn about these differences together. So, come with me on this journey, and let's learn the art of living a life full of real happiness.

Difference between happiness and Joy

Happiness is like feeling good inside for a long time. It's about being satisfied with your life. It can be the result of reaching your big goals, having people in your life who mean a lot to you, and living in a way that matches what you believe in. It's a quiet, steady feeling that stays with you, even though sometimes what's happening around you can change how you feel.

Joy is different. It's a strong, happy feeling that comes quickly and doesn't last too long. It's like when something wonderful takes you by surprise and makes you feel great all of a sudden. Joy might come from little things, like seeing a beautiful sunset or laughing with a friend. It's a feeling that comes from inside you, no matter what's going on outside.

Happiness is about feeling good for a long time, while joy is about those great moments that come and go. Both make our lives better. It's good to look for moments of joy every day. You can do this by noticing and being grateful for the good things around you. When you're thankful for the little, nice things in life, you feel joy right then. Over time, this joy can help you feel happier. Joy shows us how special the small things are and brings fun and surprise to our lives. If we keep looking for gratitude and being thankful for these moments, we build a life that's full of happiness that lasts.

Now that we know the difference between happiness and joy, let's talk about how being thankful can make both feelings stronger. Studies published in Clinical Psychology Review and the Journal of Positive Psychology found out that when people are grateful, they feel happier with their lives, have better mental health, and just feel happier overall.

How to Find Happiness

Happiness starts with feeling grateful about yourself and others. Every day, we have so many good things around us, but we often don't see them because we're too busy or we're expecting other things. When we stop complaining and start being grateful, it really changes our brain. According to the neuroscience of gratitude, practicing gratitude can stimulate two important regions in our brains: the hypothalamus, which regulates stress, and the ventral tegmental area, which plays a significant role in the brain's reward system that produces feelings of joy.

Feeling gratitude and appreciation isn't just about feeling good; it's like a positive energy that lifts us up and connects us with something bigger, whether you call it the universe, God, or your inner spirit. There's this idea called the law of attraction that says when you focus on being grateful, you'll find even more things to be thankful for, and that makes you happier. This is why every religion worldwide places great emphasis on gratitude and appreciation through various rituals. For instance: In Christianity, the Eucharist is a powerful ritual of gratitude, symbolizing the giving of thanks for the sacrifice of Jesus. In Islam, daily prayers, especially during Ramadan, serve as an expression of gratitude to Allah. Hinduism practices "puja," a ritual of devotion and thankfulness to various deities. Buddhism encourages mindfulness and meditation as a way to cultivate gratitude and inner peace. Jewish traditions include prayers of gratitude like the "Modeh Ani " recited upon waking.

Now, let's try a simple thing you can do to bring these ideas into your life and make a "Snapshot of Happiness."

Snapshot of Happiness

"Snapshot of Happiness" is a simple thing you can do anytime, anywhere. It's about noticing the good things in your life and around you. When you do this, you start to see more good things and fewer problems. This idea comes from the law of attraction, which says that when you focus on being thankful and happy about the good stuff, you'll get even more of it. Here's how you can do "Snapshot of Happiness"

Start by being in the moment. It doesn't matter if you're walking, driving, or getting ready to sleep. Put aside worries about what's coming up or what's already happened. Look around you like you're seeing everything for the first time. Find something that makes you feel warm inside or makes you smile. It could be a pretty flower, someone being nice, a happy memory, or just a little thing that makes your day better. Think of this moment as a 'snapshot' and say 'thank you' in your head or write it down. This shows you're grateful and tells the Universe you want more good stuff like this. Doing this reminds us that loving and being thankful are connected, and they bring good energy into our lives. Keep looking for and being thankful for the good things, and you'll start to see even more to be thankful for. This way, you're asking for more happiness and less trouble in your life.

"Snapshot of Happiness" isn't just about changing how you think; it's something you do that can change your everyday life. It helps you see the world's beauty and good things. Keep doing it, and you'll see your life fill up with these happy 'snapshots,' making a circle of joy and thanks. This simple practice instantly connects you to higher frequencies, where you can attract more happiness, peace, relaxation, and goodness into your life.

Lesson.2: Embracing Self-Love and Gratitude

"You yourself, as much as anybody in the entire universe, deserve your love and affection." - Buddha

Do you ever feel hurt by little things that someone does or says? Do you often feel stressed or anxious about your life? Do you dislike the way you look, your height, your colour, your voice or anything else about yourself? Do you seek love from someone else instead of from yourself? Do you neglect your health, your hobbies, your dreams or your passions? Do you complain about everything and compare yourself to others? Do you think that other people are doing better than you or have more than you? Do you depend too much on someone else for your happiness and well-being?

If you answered yes to any of these questions, then you lack self-love. Self-love is the purest and highest form of energy, but often we forget its power or we are not aware of this truth. Every moment when we feel happy and joyful, we actually feel loved. We feel love for a person, thing, act, or situation. But in today's world, we have time for everyone and everything but we don't have time for ourselves. We think about ourselves but mostly in a negative way. We ignore all the positive things happening in our lives.

Self-love means loving yourself unconditionally, regardless of your flaws or imperfections. It means accepting yourself for who you are and what you can do. It means respecting yourself and setting healthy boundaries with others, and taking care of yourself physically, mentally, emotionally, and spiritually. Self-love is the first step to experiencing the life-changing power of gratitude and appreciation because you cannot feel grateful until you love yourself.

As Wayne Dyer (American writer and motivational speaker) said: "If you don't love yourself, nobody will. Not only that, you won't be good at loving anyone else. Loving starts with the self." When you love yourself, you will also be able to love others better. You will be more compassionate, generous, and kind. You will be more confident, creative, and productive. You will be more joyful, peaceful, and grateful.

Past Trauma or abuse, bad childhood experiences, lack of self-compassion, external validation is some of the reasons why we lack self-love. But the good news is that self-love is not something that is fixed or permanent; it is something that can be learned and cultivated with the power of gratitude and appreciation. Self-love is a choice that we make every day, every moment, every breath.

We think that others have better lives than us or are more beautiful than us. We don't appreciate our own uniqueness and value. This story teaches us to love ourselves as we are and be grateful for what we have. It teaches us that we are enough just as we are; we don't need to change anything about ourselves to be worthy of love and happiness.

"To fall in love with yourself is the first secret to happiness."
- Robert Morley

As Haemin Sunim (one of the most influential Zen Buddhist teachers and writers in the world) said: "You are enough just as you are. Each emotion you feel, everything in your life, everything you do or do not do… where you are and who you are right now is enough. It is perfect. You are perfect enough."

Step-by-Step Guide About How to Love Yourself Unconditionally:

Step 1: Accept Yourself Unconditionally: Accept what there is about you: your strengths, weaknesses, and quirks. Be at peace with your uniqueness, who and what you are, and that you are worthy. Self-acceptance creates a base for self-love.

Step 2: Forgive Yourself: Forget mistakes or regrets of the past. Self-reproach stops one from moving forward. Permit yourself to forgive yourself for something you regret, as you would forgive your beloved friend for that same mistake because this is an essential part of self-compassion. When you let yourself forgive, you let go of guilt and open up healing and growth.

Step 3: Do Not Compare: Your journey is unique. Comparing yourself to others undermines your progress. Rather than looking at others, focus on personal growth. Instead of comparing and feeling bad about it, pat yourself on the back: Realize that everybody has their journey, and uniqueness paves the way for self-appreciation.

Step 4: Take Good Care of Yourself: Nurtures your physical health through proper diet, exercise, and adequate rest. Taking care of your body is an act of self-love, contributing to your overall well-being and happiness.

Step 5: Your Happiness and Peace of Mind Should Come Firs: Don't forget to self-care. Do something that gives you peace of mind and keeps you happy. Taking care of your mental and emotional well-being is crucial for the growth of self-love. Things that add to the energy and other positive domains of well-being are essential.

Gratitude and appreciation, when mixed with self-love, can completely change things for the better. When you like and accept yourself, you spread good vibes that bring more good things and happiness into your life easily. Your confidence shines brightly, attracting success, true friendships, and love.

This change makes things feel smooth and easy. Problems don't seem so bad anymore, relationships get better, and you naturally feel happy most of the time. Thankfulness and appreciation open the door to a life where every moment is filled with joy and feels good.

By practicing gratitude, even for the little things, you open yourself up to a life that's amazing and wonderful. Appreciating yourself and the world around you creates a wave effect, making the good feelings inside you and around you even stronger. This positive energy effortlessly changes your life for the better, bringing new chances, strengthening connections, and making every day feel full and rich.

Choosing to be thankful and appreciative isn't just an option; it's a chance to see the magic happen when you open your heart to how beautiful life is. It's the key to unlocking a life where happiness, good things, and feeling good aren't faraway dreams but things you experience every day.

"Peace comes from within. Do not seek it without." - Gautama Buddha

Lesson. 3: Gratitude and Belief

"Believe you deserve it, and the universe will serve it."
—Amanda Frances

How do some people achieve amazing things in life without much effort, while others struggle to get by? How can someone with no qualifications land a dream job, or someone without talent run a successful business? The answer is simple: it all depends on their beliefs and their ability to be grateful for them.

Beliefs are the foundation of everything we do and everything we become. They are the essence of our faith, and our faith determines our reality. As the Bhagavad Gita Chapter 17:3 says: "Faith is the essence of everything, and it is the support of all." "Man becomes what his faith is."

This means that whatever we believe in, we attract into our lives. Our beliefs shape our character and our destiny. Different religions have different beliefs about God; some believe that God exists in idols, some believe that God is formless, some believe that God is everywhere, and some believe that God is in one place. Who is right? Everyone is right with their own beliefs. God, who is a master creator of everything, always gives things based on beliefs because beliefs are the direct clear vibrational message that reaches God. As we already understand the game of Vibrations, it is also important to know that we radiate vibration based on our beliefs. When we have positive beliefs, we send out positive vibrations that attract positive outcomes. When we have negative beliefs, we send out negative vibrations that attract negative outcomes.

One of the most powerful examples of how beliefs can change our reality is the story of Jesus and the blind man. As Luke Chapter 18:25 says:

One day, as Jesus was coming near Jericho, there was a blind man sitting on the side of the road, asking for help. When he heard a crowd passing by, he asked what was going on. Someone told him that Jesus of Nazareth was passing by. The blind man called out to Jesus, saying, “Jesus, Son of David, please show me mercy!” Jesus heard him and stopped. He asked the blind man, “What can I do for you?” The blind man replied, “Lord, I want to be able to see again.” Jesus said to him, "You will regain your sight. Your faith has healed you." Immediately, the blind man could see again, and he started following Jesus, praising God.

This story shows us how the blind man’s faith in Jesus healed his physical condition. He believed that Jesus could restore his vision, and he received what he believed in. His faith was stronger than his fear or doubt. Like this, there are also thousands of stories where people change their situation by their beliefs.

The Art of Manifesting Through Beliefs

Manifesting what we want isn't just about believing; it's also about feeling grateful and appreciating it too. Belief sets the stage, but gratitude and appreciation are like the fuel that pushes our desires into reality. They help you give more and more clear and positive vibration to the universe of what you want. So, believe in what you want, feel grateful for it, and express appreciation through your words. That combination will definitely manifest your desire into reality.

Imagine you really want a car. Instead of stressing about how to get the money, trust the Universe. Picture yourself with the car you want, feeling happy, excited, and grateful. Imagine every detail, from the colour to the design. By focusing on this vision, feeling grateful for it, and appreciating it, you're sending positive vibrations to the Universe to attract what you want because the Universe understands vibrations rather than the literal words you speak.

Beliefs in Action

When we started our company, we mostly got small clients, deals ranging from 1000 to 5000 rupees, because of the kind of services we offered. But we wanted bigger clients, those dealing in lakhs, which seemed like a far-off dream then. But something changed in our thinking. Can you guess what it was?

I changed how our team thought about things. No matter how small the deal was, we decided to believe that every 1000-rupee deal was like a one-lakh deal, and every 10,000-rupee deal was a 10-lakh deal accomplished. We'd be really thankful to the Universe for every success. For every deal we started to feel gratitude and appreciate it. As we kept doing this, something amazing happened. In a short time, we got a big one-lakh rupee deal. After that, things changed a lot for us. We started getting deals worth lakhs every single day.

This change showed us how powerful gratitude, appreciation and beliefs are. It made us sure that we attract what we truly believe in. With this understanding, I got better at noticing and changing my thoughts whenever I felt something was wrong. By changing my mindset and being really thankful, I saw reality changing in response. It's something I do a lot, being grateful from the bottom of my heart.

How to Change Your Self-Limiting Beliefs?

Changing beliefs is a process that starts with awareness. Identify limiting beliefs and replace them with empowering thoughts by repeating affirmations consistently. Consistency, repetition, and integrating gratitude and appreciation into this practice will reshape you limiting beliefs. This process requires a willingness to let go of the old and embrace the new. Once you do this, you will discover the power of your beliefs and the power of your faith. You will realize that you are the creator of your life, and you can manifest anything you want.

"Whatever the mind can conceive and believe, it can achieve." – Napoleon Hill

Lesson.4: The Foundation of a strong relationship

"Gratitude is the open door to abundance and the key to a lasting relationship." - Louise Hay

Have you ever seen couples who argue all the time, or houses where bad feelings seem to stick around? It happens a lot these days. Every thought we have has energy, and when our minds are full of grumbling and bad feelings, it makes a place nobody wants to be. This often makes us look for happiness outside our homes, at hotels, parties, or on trips far away, desperately searching for peace we can't find at home.

Relationship Challenge

Have you ever thought about why people get less patient and relationships fall apart? This isn't just happening between husbands and wives, it's everywhere! The reason is because we forget who we really are and the good things our parents and teachers told us. We've all read books like the Gita, Bible, and Quran, and they all say the same thing: be thankful and appreciate what you have.

Being thankful and appreciating things is the foundation of love, the glue that holds everyone together in this big world. Often, the reason relationships are hard is because of the things we do. We don't even realize it, but we act in ways that make things worse instead of better. When problems come up, we only focus on what's wrong and complain. These bad thoughts just make more bad thoughts and complaints. This cycle can get worse and worse, leading to big fights, breakups, or even worse.

We get so caught up in complaining that we overlook the good in others. We forget to appreciate even when we see positive things. Instead of checking our own thoughts, we tend to blame the other person. We justify our negative thoughts by believing the other person deserves our complaints or that their actions warrant negativity.

It's important to recognize this pattern and shift our focus. Instead of dwelling on complaints, fostering positive thoughts and appreciation can transform relationships for the better.

Remember gratitude and love—two powerful pillars that can help tackle the hurdles in a relationship. Picture the last time you truly appreciated your partner from the depths of your heart, not just to express love but genuinely, with raw emotions. Do you find yourself grateful for the little things they do? It could be something as simple as ensuring you sleep comfortably or waking you up on time, maybe preparing coffee or breakfast—small acts that mean the world.

Gratitude and appreciation, when woven into the fabric of a relationship, have the power to make it resilient. Regardless of the present situation, infusing gratitude into your connection works like magic. It gradually transforms your partner, and this ongoing practice acts as a remedy for the challenges in your relationship.

When you express appreciation, do it with all your emotions. Take a moment to fathom the impact of those small acts before you express gratitude. The more you appreciate your partner, the stronger your bond becomes. Remember, a relationship thriving on appreciation and gratitude is bound to be filled with love. Keep nurturing it, and you'll witness the transformation firsthand.

Appreciation in Action: How Gratitude Transformed My Relationship

Practicing gratitude can truly transform relationships, including the way we perceive our partners and their actions. It's about shifting our focus from what we might see as shortcomings to appreciating their positive attributes and gestures.

Gratitude unlocks the fullness of life. It turns what we have into enough, and more. It turns denial into acceptance, chaos into order, confusion into clarity... It turns problems into gifts, failures into success, the unexpected into perfect timing, and mistakes into important events. Gratitude makes sense of our past, brings peace for today and creates a vision for tomorrow." - Melody Beattie

In my own experience, when I was facing challenges in my relationship, I turned to gratitude. I made a conscious effort to acknowledge and appreciate all the wonderful things about my partner. I started by jotting down everything I admired about her and even included the qualities I hoped she would embody. Each day, I expressed gratitude for her actions, big or small, by writing them in a diary. Over just 20 days, this practice completely shifted how I viewed her. I began to see her as incredibly caring, supportive, and loving.

Through this process, something magical happened. My partner also seemed to change her perspective about me and her actions. She started acknowledging my efforts and expressing how much she valued my love. This simple yet powerful act of gratitude transformed our relationship into a more loving and understanding one.

"When gratitude becomes an essential foundation in our lives, miracles start to appear everywhere." - Emmanuel Dagher

Gratitude in relationships is linked to better mental health. According to a study published in the Journal of Personality and Social Psychology, people who express gratitude tend to experience fewer symptoms of depression and anxiety. In relationships, this can translate to a healthier emotional environment.

Researchers at the University of Georgia found that expressing gratitude towards a partner leads to a higher level of commitment in the relationship. Partners who feel appreciated are more likely to invest in the relationship and remain committed to each other over time.

The key was focusing on the positive aspects, appreciating even the smallest gestures, and genuinely feeling thankful for them. It's incredible how this practice of gratitude not only changed how I saw my partner but also how she perceived me. It's a testament to the remarkable power of gratitude in relationships.

How to make any relationship strong

Remember Special Days: In nurturing strong and healthy relationships, it's vital to remember and celebrate not only the big milestones like birthdays and anniversaries but also the everyday moments that often go unnoticed. These simple yet profound acts of appreciation can be transformative, both for you and your loved ones. When you make an effort to create happiness in your relationship through gestures of gratitude and appreciation, you infuse it with love and joy. Even the tiniest act of kindness can be a powerful antidote to negativity, clearing away past grievances and strengthening the bonds between you. Maya Angelou wisely said, "People will forget what you said, people will forget what you did, but people will never forget how you made them feel." By consistently making your loved ones feel appreciated, you create a strong and lasting connection that transcends special occasions.

Encourage and Support: When you actively support your partner's goals and dreams, you're demonstrating gratitude for their ambitions and aspirations. By being their cheerleader, you're acknowledging their desires and showing appreciation for their growth and individuality within the relationship. It fosters an environment of mutual respect and admiration.

Apologize When Necessary: Apologizing sincerely when you've made a mistake shows your partner that you value and appreciate the relationship enough to acknowledge your faults. It's a form of gratitude for their understanding and forgiveness. It signifies that you respect their feelings and care about their well-being, reinforcing the bond of trust and respect.

Say "Thank You": These two simple words hold immense power. Expressing gratitude through "thank you" demonstrates appreciation for even the smallest gestures. It acknowledges your partner's efforts, reaffirming that you don't take them for granted. It creates a positive cycle of appreciation and acknowledgment in the relationship.

Compliments: Regularly offering genuine compliments to your partner shows appreciation for their qualities, efforts, and appearance. It communicates that you notice and value their positive attributes, contributing to their self-esteem and reinforcing their importance in your life.

Celebrate Achievements: Acknowledging and celebrating your partner's achievements, whether big or small, demonstrates gratitude for their hard work and dedication. It shows that you take joy in their successes and that you're genuinely proud of their accomplishments, contributing to a supportive and encouraging relationship atmosphere.

Express Feelings: Sharing your emotions openly and honestly with your partner is a form of gratitude for their understanding and support. It creates a space for intimacy and trust, allowing both partners to feel appreciated and valued for their vulnerabilities and strengths.

Always feel grateful: In every relationship, gratitude is like sunlight—it nurtures love and helps it grow. Remembering to appreciate each other's small efforts and saying 'thank you' can make a big difference. It's a journey, not just a one-time thing. Keep thanking, keep appreciating, and watch your relationship grow stronger every day."

Gratitude is the secret ingredient to a happy relationship, not only between partners but also among family members and friends. Whether it's your spouse, sister, mother, father, or any loved one, expressing gratitude strengthens bonds and helps you build deeper connections to avoid any kind of problems. Keep saying 'thank you,' appreciate the small things, and watch your love flourish. It's an ongoing journey—a little gratitude goes a long way in making your relationship stronger."

Gratitude is the healthiest of all human emotions. The more you express gratitude for what you have, the more likely you will have even more to express gratitude for." - Zig Ziglar

Lesson. 5: Finding Joy in Nature

"The world is full of beauty; see it. Smell it. Taste it. Touch it. Feel it."
- George Bernard Shaw

Imagine you wake up in the morning, open your eyes, and see total darkness—no light. You want to breathe, but there's no air. You reach for water, but it's gone. Worried, you try to leave your home to find help, but you can't move. I know this won't happen, but think about it: isn't it amazing that every second, the most important things for life are there for us, free of charge? Nature is kind—many things happen every second to keep you alive. But we often forget this, focusing on our problems and missing the joy of life.

Now, imagine the same scene differently. You open your eyes and feel happy to be alive. You're glad to breathe easily and thankful for what nature and God provide. You stay grateful all day and go to bed content and excited for tomorrow.

Life is amazing, and if we're healthy and can follow our dreams, we're very lucky. Seeing and appreciating the good in life brings more blessings. Often, we worry about owning things—'this is mine, that is mine,' but nothing truly belongs to us. Everything is part of nature, and we are too. The products we use, even seeds, are really from nature and God. We don't create anything; we just use what nature and the universe give us. So, since everything we have is a gift from nature, why not appreciate its abundance?

Nature talks to us in many ways—through the wind, the colours, and the quiet moments. But we're often too busy to listen. If we take time to connect with nature, we'll find so much more. People who are thankful for nature get more good things from it. When we really listen to nature and feel thankful for what it gives us, it shares more special things with us. It's like a secret that nature shares with those who stop and appreciate its story.

"Nature is the source of all true knowledge. She has her own pure and eternal truth; if you can learn it, you will have found the key to universal wisdom." - Ralph Waldo Emerson

Being grateful for nature and appreciating it is the first duty we have as human beings. By acknowledging the beauty and importance of our natural environment, we develop a sense of responsibility to protect and preserve it. This gratitude not only enhances our well-being but also inspires us to take meaningful actions toward sustainable living.

To embrace the incredible power of nature, you can start by recognizing the everyday blessings it provides, feeling grateful for them, and appreciating them. For instance, you can say:

- I'm so grateful for the sunlight that brightens our days, filling them with warmth and light.
- I appreciate the gentle breezes that kiss our cheeks and bring freshness to the air.
- I'm thankful for the green trees that provide shade and beauty, making our surroundings vibrant and calm.
- I cherish the blooming flowers that add colour and fragrance to our lives, spreading joy with their presence.
- Moreover, I'm grateful for the clear blue skies that greet us each morning, reminding us of the vastness and possibilities of the world.
- I also give thanks for the soothing sound of raindrops on the roof, bringing nourishment and comfort to the Earth.
- Lastly, I appreciate the quiet moments when I can listen to the songs of birds, a reminder of the simple, natural joys that surround us each day.

Practicing gratitude and appreciation for nature's gifts—the sun's warmth, the gentle breezes, the trees, and colourful flowers—opens our eyes to life's simple joys. Each part of nature connects us to the universe's rhythm. When we treasure these everyday wonders, we discover wisdom and endless joy. Through gratitude and appreciation, find happiness and a stronger bond with nature's kindness.

Lesson 6: Gratitude for a better physical & mental health

Mindful Eating

"Food is a gift. Respect it and eat it with joy." - A thought from Indian scriptures

Studies show that the average person spends about 3 hours and 15 minutes each day on their smartphones. Shockingly, about 60% of this time is spent on social media or gaming apps, causing many distractions. These tech activities often pull our focus away from the present moment, affecting our ability to fully engage in activities, including something as basic as eating. As a result, mealtime has become just another task we rush through, often without really noticing the food we're eating or the signals our bodies are sending us.

The effects of this rushed eating can be serious. When we are busy with other things while eating, we lose touch with the experience of nourishment. Research shows that distracted eating can lead to overeating, as we fail to notice when we're full. This can lead to weight gain and various health problems. Moreover, rushing through meals keeps us from enjoying the pleasure and satisfaction that comes from savouring each bite and being mindful of the nourishment our bodies receive.

What is Mindful Eating?

Mindful eating is based on mindfulness, which is a Buddhist concept. Mindfulness is a form of meditation that helps you recognize and cope with your emotions and physical sensations. It's used to treat many conditions, including eating disorders, depression, anxiety, and various food-related behaviours

Mindful eating is about slowing down and really noticing what you're eating. It's a break from being busy and not paying attention to our food. It means sitting down, taking a deep breath, and enjoying every bite of our meal. When we eat mindfully, we're not just eating; we're there with our food, tasting and enjoying it fully. It's about feeling thankful for our food and where it comes from.

Being grateful is a big part of mindful eating. It means to think about where our food came from and all the work that went into it. We think about the farmers, the people who picked and brought the food to us, the cooks, and everyone else who helped. Saying 'thank you' before we eat helps us feel connected to all these people and thankful for all the food we have.

Mindful eating also means being thankful for the food itself. We take time to look at its colours and shapes, to smell its scents, and to taste its Flavors. We think about how much care went into making each dish. We might even say 'thank you' to a higher power for giving us such good food to eat. This makes eating a special time, not just something we do because we have to. It's a way to feel more connected to the world and to enjoy our food even more. Research has shown that mindful eating can lead to greater psychological wellbeing, increased pleasure when eating, and body satisfaction.

My Journey Towards Mindful Eating

My journey towards mindful eating began with the profound insights found in the book 'The Science of Being Well.' It detailed not just what to eat and when, but also how to eat mindfully. When I started practicing these teachings, I noticed a big change in how I experienced food. For the first time, I really enjoyed the Flavors of my meals and realized how complex and delicious each dish was. Adding gratitude to my meals and focusing completely on eating made a big difference.

Since I started eating mindfully, I make sure to give myself enough time for each meal. Sometimes, I close my eyes to enjoy the taste even more. This way of eating has made me excited for every meal and brought me a lot of happiness. Enjoying my food mindfully has opened up a new kind of happiness for me.

"When we feed ourselves with mindfulness, we are nourishing our entire being." - Jon Kabat-Zinn

Thich Nhat Hanh says, 'When you eat mindfully, you become more present, more appreciative, and more content with the simple joy of nourishing yourself.' This gratitude changes things; it fills our meals with love, joy, and positive energy. When you eat mindfully, this magic happens, making not just your body, but also your heart and spirit feel good. The love and joy you feel mix with the food, and this deep connection stays with you all day, making your life full of joy. Mindful eating is more than just eating; it's a chance to be thankful, to love, and to find lasting happiness.

In Indian culture, saying prayers before eating is very important. It's a way to show respect for the food, the work that went into making it, and to be thankful for it. Keeping this tradition is important. It reminds us to stop, think, and be thankful, which makes every meal special.

"Mindful eating is an invitation to discover a whole new world of eating pleasure." - Jan Chozen Bays

To sum up, mindful eating is not just about the food we eat; it's about taking care of our mind, body, and soul. When we eat with mindfulness, thankfulness, and appreciation, we make eating a peaceful and happy time. Let's enjoy this way of eating, cherish every bite, and remember the journey our food has taken. Mindful eating can lead us to not just feeling full, but also to joy, thankfulness, and a good life."

"Cultivate the habit of being grateful for every good thing that comes to you, and to give thanks continuously." - Ralph Waldo Emerson

Make your water work for you

"A drop of water, if it could write out its own history, would explain the universe to us." - Lucy Larcom

Water is the essence of life, a gift from the Universe that nurtures and sustains us. Our world is brimming with this precious element, flowing in rivers, filling oceans, and falling from the sky as rain. It's the source of vitality that keeps us alive. In my view, water is akin to 'amrit,' a sacred elixir mentioned in Hindu beliefs, and I believe it embodies the presence of God among us. Scientific studies even suggest that water can respond to our thoughts and emotions. Personally, I've experienced its power through water manifestation techniques, where my desires manifest with its help.

This lesson emphasizes the incredible significance of water in our lives. It's more than just a substance; it's a vital force that deserves our gratitude and appreciation. I engage with water in a deeply personal way. I speak to it, drink it with reverence and gratitude, seeing it as both medicine and a source of happiness.

Gratitude and appreciation towards water are transformative. They shape our connection with this life-giving element, making our bond stronger and more meaningful. When we express thankfulness for water, it reciprocates in ways that bring joy and fulfilment to our lives.

Through this lesson, I aim to showcase the magic of water and how our relationship with it can elevate our existence. Its role in our lives goes beyond quenching our thirst; it's a profound entity that deserves our reverence and acknowledgment. Embracing gratitude and appreciation towards water can bring immense happiness and blessings into our lives.

Why Water Affirmation?

Water affirmations connect us deeply with this essential element, allowing us to honour its significance and express gratitude for its presence in our lives. By affirming positive thoughts about water, we infuse it with our intentions and emotions, recognizing the power of our thoughts in influencing its energy. This practice amplifies the positive effects of water on our bodies and minds, fostering a deeper connection. Regularly practicing water affirmations aligns us with life's flow and enables us to manifest our desired lives. Each sip or interaction with water becomes a moment for our intentions to be heard and acted upon. I have given some affirmations and you create new or customize these as per your needs. You can practice at least one every time before drinking the water.

Below are 5 affirmations
"I'm immensely grateful for this pure water, brimming with love and joy. Its purity nourishes me, fulfilling my wishes, and I'm grateful for its abundance."

"As water flows through me, I channel its cleansing power, spreading healing energy throughout the world."

"Every sip fills me with the vibrant energy of life force, revitalizing my body and spirit."

"My body is a sacred temple, and I honour it by nourishing it with this pure and sacred drink."
"With deep gratitude, I drink in the knowledge that the universe abundantly provides for all my needs."

Water is not just a life-giving elixir; it's pure magic in our lives. Its power transcends our understanding, and its presence is deeply woven into the fabric of our existence. Once we initiate a conversation with water, acknowledging its lively spirit and understanding its significance as the essence of life, we unlock a profound partnership. Water, ever responsive and alive, listens to our words in its own silent language and responds in ways beyond our imagination.

As we continue to embrace water with gratitude, recognizing its inherent vitality, we discover a constant companion—a partner that's not just around us but within us. The journey of connecting with water opens doors to a realm of inexplicable wonders. It's an ongoing conversation that reveals the boundless power of this essential element. Let us cherish this incredible relationship with water, for it is indeed a source of life, a healer of spirits, and an eternal friend on our journey.

"A drop of water, if it could write out its own history, would explain the universe to us." - Lucy Larcom

Lesson. 7: Ways through which you can practice gratitude

"Practice does not make perfect. Only perfect practice makes perfect."- Vince Lombardi (American Football Coach)

Now that you have discovered how powerful gratitude can be, let's understand how to practice it in your daily life. The more you practice gratitude in a perfect way, the more you will feel it in your heart. And the more you feel it, the more you will see it in your life.

Let me tell you a story which is very popular in Indian churches. Once, a Christian teacher visited a village where he explained to the villagers a verse from the Bible in which Jesus said, "Truly I tell you, if you have faith as small as a mustard seed, you can say to this mountain, 'Move from here to there,' and it will move. Nothing will be impossible for you.' (Matthew 17:20-21). A lady named Sunita Devi, who was listening to him, was deeply troubled by the mountain in front of her house. She decided to pray and move the mountain. After the teacher left, she went to her house, locked her doors and windows, and began to ask God repeatedly to move the mountain.

After two minutes of praying, she got up and opened her window to check if the mountain had disappeared, but it was still there. She prayed again for another two minutes and looked outside, but the mountain remained in place. She prayed for a third time and looked outside, only to find the mountain still in its original location. Sunita smiled and said, 'I already knew that it would not happen.'

What do you think was missing in this story? Why did Sunita's prayers not work? You see, God, the source of the universe, communicates not just through words or languages like English, Hindi, French, Telugu, or any other, but through your vibration - what you are radiating through your thoughts and feelings in your heart. Just like in this story, Sunita was asking God to move the mountain, but in her heart, she felt it was impossible, that it would not happen, that it was too big and too heavy. Consequently, she received what she was feeling in her heart.

The same principle applies when it comes to practicing gratitude. You have to feel gratitude deeply in your heart; otherwise, you will not achieve the best results. It should not be a mere word or a gesture. The more you feel it, the more it will benefit you because your feelings and thoughts are like a universal language that the universe or God understands. You have to feel grateful for everything, even for the things that seem small or insignificant. For example, when you express gratitude for food, you must also feel grateful from your heart for the person who prepared the food, the ingredients used, the farmer who cultivated the crops, and every person and thing involved in bringing those ingredients to you. Practicing gratitude has no meaning if you can't feel it in your heart.

Blessings Book

"Gratitude is a powerful catalyst for happiness. It's the spark that lights a fire of joy in your soul." – Amy Collette

You are surrounded by blessings. Just take a moment and look around you. You have so much to appreciate in your life. You are alive and breathing, you have a home and food, you have family and friends, you have talents and passions, you have dreams and goals, and much more. You are a unique and wonderful creation of God, and He loves you unconditionally. Sometimes, we get caught up in the problems and challenges that we face, and we forget to see the bigger picture and the positive possibilities. We tend to dwell on the negative aspects, and ignore all the positive ones. We let the problems overwhelm us, and we lose our faith and hope. This is where a blessings book also known as a gratitude journal can make a difference in your life. A blessings book or a gratitude journal is a simple way of expressing your gratitude for all the good things in your life. You can write down daily or weekly what you are thankful for, what made you and your family happy, what inspired you, what touched your heart, or what lifted your spirit. You can also include quotes, scriptures, prayers, affirmations, or anything else that helps you connect with God and His goodness.

By doing this, you will shift your perspective and your energy. You will see the solutions instead of the obstacles. You will see the opportunities instead of the limitations. You will see miracles instead of mistakes. You will see how God is working in your life, and how He is blessing you every day. You will feel more joy, peace, love, and happiness. You will attract more abundance, success, health, and harmony. You will become more positive, optimistic, encouraging, and spiritual.

Gratitude changes everything. It aligns you with your true source of abundance and happiness. It attracts more good things to you. When you feel like things are not going your way, just pause and take a deep breath. And then think of all the reasons you have to be grateful. Write them down in your blessings book. And then thank God for all His gifts and grace.

This practice, it's been my guiding light for a year now. My Gratitude Journal isn't just a notebook; it's a conduit to the divine. Each time I scribble down what lights up my life, it feels like a direct conversation with the universe, a heartfelt chat with the goodness that surrounds me. I seek out those 4 or 5 moments in my day that truly resonate, moments that sparkle even amidst life's challenges, reminding me that gratitude outshines any adversity. And it's not confined to today; I sketch out the potential for tomorrow, envisioning ways to make it even brighter.

Morning or night, whether after a serene meditation or just before drifting into sleep, I open this journal. It's my personal energy recharge, a pill of motivation, and a cup overflowing with appreciation. This isn't just about jotting down words; it's about nurturing a profound bond with gratitude that fills me with unending joy and contentment. This ritual isn't merely a record; it's a transformative journey towards a more abundant, vibrant life. What's fascinating is that I've discovered the power of including my future plans and wishes in my Gratitude Journal. I write them down with such fervour, feeling grateful for these forthcoming blessings as if they've already manifested. And here's the incredible part: almost miraculously, whatever I've written in my journal often materializes in my reality within a few days. It's as if the act of gratitude and visualization propels these aspirations into existence. This practice has consistently shown me that what I believe and appreciate tends to manifest in my life.

You can do this by writing down what you are excited about for the next day, week, month, or year. You can write down what you want to achieve, experience, learn, or share. You can write down who you want to meet, help, or collaborate with. You can write down how you want to feel, grow, or contribute.

By doing this, you are sending a powerful message to the universe that you are ready for more good things to come your way. You are telling God that you trust His plan for your life and that you are open to His guidance and grace.

You are also creating a positive expectation for yourself that will motivate you to take action towards your goals and dreams. You are setting yourself up for success and happiness.

So, start today by writing down what you are excited about for tomorrow or next week or next year. Write it down in your blessings book or gratitude journal as if it has already happened or is happening right now.

For example:
- I am so excited that I got an interview for my dream job today.
- I am so happy that I finished writing my first book this week.
- I am so proud that I have built a successful business.
- I am so proud that I have a YouTube channel with 10 million subscribers.
- I am so amazed that I travelled to my favourite destination this year.
- I am so blessed that I made a positive impact on someone's life today.
- I am so grateful that I am following my passion and making a good living out of it.

Write it down with enthusiasm and emotion. Write it down with gratitude and faith. And then watch how your life changes for the better. Gratitude is not only a feeling. It's also a power. Use it wisely and generously.

By blending the gratitude for today's blessings with the dreams and aspirations for tomorrow in your Blessings Book or Gratitude Journal, you're not just writing; you're declaring your readiness to welcome the abundance waiting to unfold. These written aspirations are your way of affirming faith in the universe's plan, extending an invitation for its guidance and grace to illuminate your path. Each entry becomes more than mere words on paper; it becomes a radiant beacon, lighting the way to a future filled with success and joy. It's about infusing those words with the pulsating energy of gratitude and unwavering faith, setting in motion a force that shapes the reality you envision.

Therefore, let this cherished Blessings Book or Gratitude Journal become your sacred space—a fusion of dreams and gratitude—a vessel that breathes life into your aspirations.

Embrace it with zeal, and witness the tapestry of your life unfurl in exquisite and unexpected ways through the enchanting power of gratitude.

"Gratitude unlocks the fullness of life. It turns what we have into enough, and more. It turns denial into acceptance, chaos to order, confusion to clarity. It can turn a meal into a feast, a house into a home, a stranger into a friend." – Melody Beattie

A Jar full of goodness

Do you know why we tend to focus on the negative things in life, even when they are not that big or important? Well, it's because of our brains. Our brains are wired to pay more attention to the bad stuff than the good stuff. This is due to evolution. Our ancestors had to survive in harsh environments where they faced many dangers and threats. So, remembering the negative situations, such as predators and hazards, was more useful than remembering the positive ones, like finding food.

But guess what? We're lucky now. We're much safer. We don't have to worry about being eaten by a lion or falling off a cliff. We can relax, enjoy, and appreciate what is good in our lives. And we can train our brains to do that too. How? With a Gratitude Jar.

A gratitude jar is where you put slips of paper with things that you are grateful for. You can use any jar that you like and decorate it as you wish. It helps you collect and store your gratitude in a tangible way. You can see how much gratitude you have accumulated over time and how it fills up your jar.

How to make and use a gratitude jar:

1- Find a jar that you like. It can be big or small, glass or plastic, plain or fancy. It's up to you.

2- Decorate your jar as you wish. You can use stickers, ribbons, paint, or anything else that makes it look appealing to you.

3- Label your jar with something like "Gratitude Jar," "Thank You Jar," or "Blessings Jar."

4- Prepare some slips of paper and a pen. You can use any paper that you have, such as sticky notes, index cards, or scrap paper. You can also use different colours or shapes of paper if you want.

5- "Take a moment to centre yourself and reflect on experiences, moments, or people that have brought immense joy, comfort, or lessons into your life. Write down these instances on individual slips of paper, pouring your heart into each one. Recall the feelings, emotions, and the profound impact these moments had on you. Feel the warmth of appreciation and let it flow through your words. - Fold your slip of paper and put it in your jar. You can do this every day, every week, every month, or whenever you feel like it.

6- Repeat the process until your jar is full or until you want to stop.

Open your jar and read your slips of paper whenever you want to feel more grateful. You can do this on special days, such as birthdays, holidays, or anniversaries. You can also do this on regular days, such as mornings, nights, or weekends. You can also do this alone or with others.

Another way to use a gratitude jar is to write down your desires and put them in. This can help you focus on your goals, align your energy with what you want, and make it more likely to happen.

Write down your desires in the present tense, as if they have already happened. Also, write down why you are grateful for them and how they make you feel.

For example:
- I am so happy and grateful that I have my dream job because it allows me to express my talents and passions. It provides me with financial security and freedom. I have learned to work hard and smart and to enjoy what I do.

- I am so happy and grateful that I have a healthy and fit body because it gives me energy and vitality. It enhances my appearance and confidence. I have learned to take care of myself and respect my body.

Fold your slip of paper and put it in your jar. Do this as often as you want. Open your jar and read your slips whenever you want to feel more motivated, inspired, or confident. When your wish comes true, remove the slip from the jar and celebrate!

"Embracing a gratitude jar is a celebration of life's abundant blessings, big and small. As each slip fills the jar, it becomes a tangible reminder of the richness in our lives. The power of this practice doesn't just lie in the jar but in the transformation, it ignites within us. It's a daily invitation to shift our focus from the negative to the positive, from scarcity to abundance.

Through the jar, we curate a gallery of gratitude, capturing the moments that make our hearts sing. It's not just about recording events; it's about infusing each slip with heartfelt emotion, from the joy of a sunrise to the warmth of a smile. With each addition, we train our minds to seek out the good, nurturing an unwavering appreciation for life's treasures.

The jar isn't merely a repository; it's a beacon of hope, a source of inspiration. It amplifies our desires, aligning our energies with our dreams. As we pen down our aspirations, we visualize them manifesting, fuelling our motivation and steering us toward our goals. And when those desires materialize, we pluck out those slips with gratitude, celebrating the magic of manifestation.

So, let the gratitude jar be your confidant, your cheerleader, and your manifestation portal. Embrace it with open arms, nurture it with sincere appreciation, and watch as it transforms your outlook on life. Allow gratitude to guide your journey, and may your jar overflow with the goodness life abundantly offers.

Gratitude Guide: Your Daily Calendar of Positivity

"In daily life, we must see that it is not happiness that makes us grateful, but gratefulness that makes us happy." – David Steindl-Rast

Gratitude Calendar, a powerful way to start thinking about the good things you want to see each day. It helps you focus on what you're grateful for and the positive things you hope to happen, making you feel gratitude and be happier and healthier. It's more than just feeling good, it's about actively making your life better by filling your days with positivity and purpose. Using a gratitude calendar isn't just a habit, it's a way to control your experiences and feel grateful, even when things are tough.

My Experience with the Gratitude Calendar:

Adding a Gratitude Calendar to my routine has been amazing! It reminds me every hour to think about the good things I want to happen and to be thankful for what I already have, even when things are going wrong. This has really changed how I see my day and helps me set positive goals about what I want to achieve. Here are some of the sentences I've used in my Gratitude Calendar:

"Dear Shivam, Today is your extraordinary day; embrace it with gratitude."

"Hi Shivam, Feel the magic of this day and be grateful for its wonders."

"Hello Shivam, Nature's unconditional love surrounds you; cherish it with gratitude."

"My dear Shivam, stay excited; great things await you. Say 'Thank You'."

"I cherish you deeply, Shivam. I am always by your side, guiding you towards the best."

"Hi Shivam, remember to take extra care of yourself and be grateful."

"Hi Shivam, every challenge is surmountable; focus on the positives."

"Take a deep breath, Shivam. Relax, smile, and be grateful for the good things to come."

"Hi Shivam, Reflect on the blessings in your life and express gratitude."
"Hi Shivam, think about those who love you dearly and appreciate them wholeheartedly."

"My dear Shivam, Offer your gratitude to the Universe for the abundance in your life."

"Remember when I said today would be magical? Say 'Thank You' for its wonders."

"Hi Shivam, As the day concludes, embrace a relaxing and peaceful night. Be grateful."

"Hi Shivam, before you sleep, forgive yourself and others. Shower yourself with love, smile, and have a serene and fulfilling sleep, adorned with beautiful dreams."

These reminders in my calendar have significantly enhanced each day, infusing it with positivity and gratitude.

Creating Your Gratitude Calendar:

To make a gratitude calendar with Google Calendar, open the app and pick a time to set goals for the day ahead. Choose a time in the morning or night to think about what you're thankful for and the good things you want to happen. Make an event for each time slot, writing down your goals or positive thoughts for the day. For example, if you want to have more of something good in your life, write something like, "I'm thankful for all the good things coming my way today." Set these events to repeat daily so you don't forget to focus on gratitude and positive thinking. Make your goals personal to what you want to improve in your life, giving you the power to actively control your experiences.

Benefits and Impact of gratitude calendar:

Keeping a gratitude calendar can really change how you think and feel, giving you the power to actively make your life better. By setting goals for gratitude and positive outcomes, you shift your focus from what you lack to what you have, making you feel more optimistic and stronger. Consistently practicing gratitude and setting positive goals can lead to amazing changes in your thoughts, feelings, actions, and experiences. Over time, this proactive approach to gratitude can make you feel more fulfilled and happier, enriching your life in meaningful ways.

"Gratitude is the sweetest thing in a seeker's life – in all human life. If there is gratitude in your heart, then there will be tremendous sweetness in your eyes." - Sri Chinmoy

Gratitude Mantras: Simple Words to Change Your Life
The Power of Words

"Words have the power to inspire and the power to destroy."
- Nelson Mandela
Words have the power to shape our reality. They can inspire us, motivate us, and empower us. They can also limit us, discourage us, and weaken us. The words we choose to say to ourselves and others can make a huge difference in how we feel and what we achieve.

One of the most successful and influential movie stars in the world, Shahrukh Khan, knows this very well. He is known as the “King of Bollywood”, with over 3 billion fans across the globe. He has won countless awards, earned billions of dollars, and achieved his dreams of becoming a big star. But he did not start out that way. He was an outsider in the film industry, with no connections or background. He faced many rejections, failures, and challenges along the way.

How did he overcome them? How did he become the king of his own destiny? He did it by his work, his beliefs, and by using the power of words. He often said in his interview’s things like “I am the best”, “I will become a big star”, and “I have come here to rule”. He said these words with conviction and confidence, even when no one else believed in him. He said these words as a form of gratitude, as a way of thanking the universe for giving him the opportunity to pursue his passion. Knowingly or unknowingly, He said these words as a form of affirmation, as a way of programming his subconscious mind to attract success and happiness, and it worked. His words became his reality. He became what he said.

Just as Shahrukh Khan harnessed the power of words to manifest his dreams and rise above challenges, the potency of our language extends beyond personal affirmations. Gratitude mantras, infused with sincerity and intention, serve as vehicles for shaping our reality. They are not mere expressions but catalysts that channel positive vibrations, aligning our thoughts and emotions with the abundance and blessings that surround us. Much like Shahrukh Khan's unwavering conviction in his destiny, gratitude mantras possess the transformative ability to Mold our lives into a tapestry of gratitude and fulfilment.

What is the Gratitude Mantra?

Gratitude mantras are simple words or phrases that express gratitude for something or someone in our lives. They are not just statements of fact, but expressions of emotion. They are not just words, but feelings. They are not just sounds, but vibrations.

Gratitude mantras are easy to practice and can be done anytime, anywhere. All you need is your voice and your intention. You can say them aloud or silently, in the morning or at night, alone or with others. You can say them as a part of your meditation or prayer routine, or as a spontaneous expression of gratitude throughout the day.

The key is to say them with sincerity and emotion as if you really mean them and feel them. The more you say them, the more you will believe them and live with them.

Here are some gratitude mantras that you can use to change your life for the better

- I am grateful for God's abundance in my life.
- I am grateful for the positive energy that surrounds me.
- I appreciate every moment I'm given.
- Every day is a magical day.
- My life is filled with love, joy, peace, and abundance.
- I am strong, happy, rich, confident, and the best version of myself.
- I am a unique creation of this universe.
- I am the best.

- Today is my day.

Incorporating gratitude mantras into your life can be a transformative experience. These simple words have the power to reshape your reality, just as they did for Shahrukh Khan and other successful people in the world. Through the practice of gratitude mantras, you can manifest positivity, abundance, and a deeper connection with the universe. Remember, the more you say these mantras with sincerity and emotion, the more they will become a part of your reality.

During the lockdown, I stumbled upon the book 'The Power of Your Subconscious Mind,' and it sparked a profound change within me. I decided to infuse my daily life with gratitude mantras. I created a wallpaper on my phone with affirmations like 'I am smart, happy, rich, and confident.' Reading these phrases repeatedly, expressing gratitude for already embodying these qualities, seemed incongruous with my reality at the time. I had limited finances, an empty building floor in Noida, and a lack of confidence. Yet, as I persisted in my practice, a miraculous transformation began. Within two months, I founded my own company, employing over 70 team members. This extraordinary change, rooted in the power of words and gratitude, solidified my belief in their immense potential. I am convinced that embracing gratitude mantras with sincerity can create extraordinary shifts in one's life.

As witnessed in this real-life journey, the potency of gratitude mantras extends far beyond words—they are catalysts for profound change. Crafting your own mantras infused with belief and emotion can set in motion a series of remarkable events. Embrace this practice, infuse your words with sincerity, and watch in awe as your reality mirrors the vibrations you emit.

"Acknowledging the good that you already have in your life is the foundation for all abundance." - Eckhart Tolle

Meditation of Thanks

'Meditation is the soul's direct conversation with God.' - Paramahamsa Yogananda

When we meditate, we enter a deep and peaceful place within ourselves. We feel the presence of God in our soul and the harmony of all creation. We also discover the true essence of our being and the gifts we have to offer. Gratitude is one of these gifts. In the 'Meditation of Thanks', we will practice gratitude for all the miracles and blessings that fill our lives. This lesson will guide you on this amazing journey. It will inspire you to use gratitude to nourish your spirit and to appreciate the beauty in yourself and the world.

Setting Intentions:

In meditation, intentions are like guiding stars, providing clarity and focus. They help us connect with the essence of gratitude. Before starting the 'Meditation of Thanks,' take a moment to reflect on what you're grateful for. What fills your heart with appreciation? These thoughts become your intentions, shaping your meditation journey. Think of intentions as personal beacons of light, illuminating your path to deeper gratitude. They make your experience unique and meaningful. So, reflect, set your intentions, and embark on this transformative journey with an open heart.

Preparing for Meditation:

Find a peaceful and undisturbed space where you can fully immerse yourself in this heart-centred practice. Whether you choose to sit or lie down, ensure your position allows complete relaxation. Gently close your eyes and take a moment to centre yourself, focusing on the sensations in your heart. This meditation is best experienced with your senses fully engaged and by being entirely present in the moment. The deeper you feel the emotions in your heart, the more profound joy you'll receive, making it a truly heartfelt experience.

Begin with deep and intentional breathing. Inhale slowly through your nose, allowing the breath to fill your body. As you breathe in, visualize that you are drawing in a higher power, a divine energy, which nourishes and fills you with love and positivity. Feel the warmth and light of this energy as it enters your body.

Now, as you exhale through your mouth, release any tension, negative emotions, and energy that no longer serves your well-being. With each exhale, let go of stress, worries, and doubts, allowing them to dissipate into the atmosphere.

Continue this process of deep, mindful breathing. Inhale divine energy, and as you exhale, release negativity. Repeat this process for three to five breath cycles or until you feel completely present in the moment, relaxed, and connected to the heart-centred practice of gratitude and appreciation.

Begin by reflecting on your body, the miraculous vessel through which you experience life. Say to yourself, "I am truly grateful for this body. It allows me to see, to eat, to move, and to achieve anything I set my mind to."

Now, turn your thoughts to the breathtaking beauty of nature that surrounds us. Visualize the wonders of the natural world, from the vibrant colours of a sunset to the gentle rustling of leaves. Say to yourself, "I deeply appreciate the beauty of nature. It brings me joy every time I open my eyes."

Feel your connection to the universe and the grand tapestry of the cosmos. Acknowledge the magnificence of the world we inhabit. Say, "I am profoundly grateful to the universe for creating such an astonishing world."

Shift your focus to the life-giving sun, the radiant star that brightens our Earth every day. Express your gratitude, saying, "I am truly grateful to the sun for its warmth and light, nurturing all life on our planet."

Consider the life-sustaining elements that make our existence possible. Reflect on water, the source of life, and say, "I am deeply thankful for the gift of water. It nourishes my body and sustains life on Earth."

Turn your thoughts to the air you breathe, the invisible force that fills your lungs and fuels your being. Say, "I am profoundly grateful for the air. It gives me life with every breath."

Reflect on the nourishment you receive from food, the sustenance that keeps you going. Express your gratitude, saying, "I am truly thankful for the nourishing food that fuels my body and delights my senses."

Extend your appreciation to the hands that prepare your meals, the chefs and cooks who infuse love and creativity into every dish. Say, "I appreciate the people who create the delicious food I enjoy."

Consider the hardworking farmers who toil to cultivate the earth and provide us with an abundance of fresh produce. Say, "I am deeply grateful to the farmers who labour to feed us."

Appreciate all the individuals who contribute to your well-being in countless ways, from the doctors and nurses who care for your health to the teachers who share knowledge and wisdom. Say, "I am profoundly grateful for all those who support and nurture me."

In this meditation, there is no limit to the expressions of gratitude. You can continue to explore and appreciate the essential aspects of life, acknowledging the beauty in the ordinary and the extraordinary. Allow this reflection to awaken a profound sense of gratitude, enveloping your being with appreciation for the interconnected web of existence.

As this meditation comes to a close, take a moment to Savor the profound sense of gratitude and appreciation that now surrounds you. You've embarked on a journey to the heart of gratitude, and in doing so, you've unlocked the transformative power of thankfulness.

Know that this practice is always available to you, allowing you to connect with the beauty of life on a deeper level. Carry this gratitude with you, sharing it with the world and creating a more fulfilling and joyful life.

Whenever you need to rekindle your sense of appreciation, remember this meditation, and know that gratitude is a boundless source of joy and positivity.

Slowly, begin to bring your awareness back to the present moment. Wiggle your fingers and toes, gently return to your surroundings, and, when you're ready, open your eyes. You've completed the 'Meditation of Thanks,' and the light of gratitude continues to shine within you.

In this 'Meditation of Thanks,' you've embarked on a journey to awaken gratitude, infusing your existence with joy, positivity, and fulfilment. Make this meditation a regular part of your routine, allowing gratitude to become a constant presence in your life. As you nurture gratitude, it becomes a wellspring of joy, a source of positivity, and a catalyst for deeper connections with yourself and others. The power of gratitude is a lifelong companion, enriching your daily experiences and contributing to a kinder, more compassionate, and joyful world. As you open your heart to gratitude, it opens doors to a world of possibilities and countless blessings, guiding you to a life filled with purpose and contentment.

Lesson 8 Manifest your desires through Gratitude

In previous chapters, we've discussed ways to integrate gratitude into your personality. By making gratitude a part of your life, you become like a Kalpvriksha, a wish-fulfilling tree mentioned in yogic culture that is capable of creating any desire.

Whether you want a dream job, business, a fulfilling relationship, a material object, or anything else, it's all possible to manifest by developing a gratitude personality because as I mentioned before "Gratitude is like a magnet, the more you will receive to be grateful for". But in our fast-paced world, we often seek instant results of our specific desires, and the good news is: it is also possible with gratitude. If you want to manifest specific desires through gratitude, here's a step-by-step guide:

Step 1: Release Negative Vibrations

First, you must release the negative vibrations surrounding your current desire. For example, if you desire money, don't focus on negative beliefs like "I don't have money," "Money is hard to come by," or "Money is bad." These create a negative frequency that hinders manifestation.

Similarly, if you want to attract your dream job or business, remove the negativity associated with it. Don't criticize the source of your income. Avoid statements like "I have to work here under compulsion" or "This is a terrible job."

Step 2: Find the Good in Your Current Situation

Instead, start finding the good things about your current job, financial situation, or business. If you desire a better job, acknowledge the positive aspects of your current one.

Step 3: Get Specific, Feel Grateful and Appreciate

Now, write down your desires in detail. If you want a dream job, specify the salary, company, and other desired aspects. Then, visualize yourself having that job and start feeling grateful and appreciate it as if it has already happened.

Step 4: Practice Affirmations

Finally, practice affirmations as per your desires. Here are a few examples to get you started (replace "desire" with your specific goal):

"I am grateful for the abundance that is flowing into my life."
"I am open to receiving my desire."
"I am worthy of achieving my desire."
"I am on the right track to manifesting my desire."
"I trust that the universe will bring me my desire in perfect timing."

By following these steps and cultivating gratitude, you will 100% manifest your desires.
Remember, consistency and a feeling of gratitude are key!

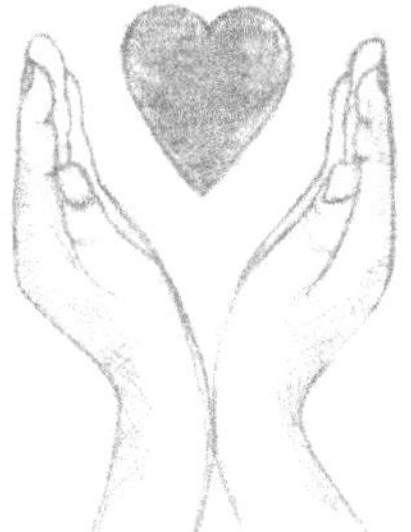

Lesson 9: Heartfelt Appreciation

"Your heart is the centre of your power. I have learned that you can create easily and effortlessly when you let your thoughts come from the loving space of the heart." (Sadhguru)

From a young age, we're told to say 'thank you' to show we're grateful when someone helps us. But many don't learn the deep meaning of these words and how to really mean them. What if there's more to this simple phrase? What if "thank you" could be a superpower?

In this lesson, we'll look closely at 'thank you' and its true importance. We'll see what this strong phrase means and how to fill it with real feeling and purpose. We want to move past just saying it out of habit and grasp the real spirit of 'Heartwarming Appreciation.'

What is Heartwarming Appreciation?

Heartwarming Appreciation' is a true and deep sense of gratitude. It's usually showing or feeling thanks in a way that makes the heart feel warm and brings joy, love, or cheer. It's often about seeing the good someone or something has done and sharing your thanks in a sincere and meaningful way. 'Heartwarming Appreciation' can be shown through words, actions, signs, or any way that truly shows the kind and touching thankfulness you feel. Also, remember: It's not necessary to show it directly to the person, and it doesn't need words to be expressed. Whenever you're truly thankful for someone and you show it with all your heart's emotions, it works. We're all connected like a big network, so whatever we feel or think about someone always gets to them.

Why Is It Important?

'Heartwarming Appreciation' is vital because it makes bonds stronger, improves happiness, inspires people, creates a good vibe, encourages giving back, helps us bounce back, better our talks, and grows a caring culture. This leads to a kinder, more helpful world.

Always keep in mind, when you thank someone or something, it must be heartfelt. If it's not felt deeply, saying thank you or showing appreciation can seem empty. To truly connect with 'Heartwarming Appreciation,' you need to be aware and thoughtful. Consider the impact of the kindness you've received, no matter how small. It might be challenging to feel at first, but with daily practice, 'Heartwarming Appreciation' will become a natural part of your life, enhancing your joy.

Every thought we have carries energy that affects us. When we choose 'Heartwarming Appreciation,' we spread positive energy, creating a joyful space for ourselves and others. As you continue on your journey of gratitude, embrace 'Heartwarming Appreciation' at every chance. Show your thanks from the heart, and watch as it transforms your world and the world around you.

"Develop an attitude of gratitude, and give thanks for everything that happens to you, knowing that every step forward is a step toward achieving something bigger and better than your current situation." - Gautama Buddha

Lesson 10 Writing a Gratitude letter to the Universe

"The Universe is always speaking to us... sending us little messages, causing coincidences and serendipities, reminding us to stop, to look around, to believe in something else, something more." - Nancy Thayer

Writing to the Universe isn't just putting pen to paper, it's like a magic trick that changes you for the better. It's a way to tell the universe, with all your heart, how thankful you are, even for the things you don't quite understand. This can make amazing things happen in your life, like putting you in perfect rhythm with the universe's flow. Whether you need help, want to say thanks, or wish for something special, this simple and honest practice is super powerful. It's almost like a magic spell! When your heart overflows with love and thanks for the universe, you become super positive and open to good things. This connection with something bigger isn't about religion; it's for everyone, no matter what you believe in. Whether you call it God, Allah, Shiva, or something else, it's all about knowing there's a powerful force looking out for you. In my heart, I believe these are all names for the same amazing thing, just with different words because of culture or religion. It's the pure thankfulness and love that make the magic happen, opening the door to connect with the universe's amazing energy.

The Universe Listens

When you fill your heart with gratitude and love for this bigger force, you start to see how the universe lines things up for you. Your thoughts, dreams, and wishes become one with the universe's energy, bringing things into your life that make your soul happy. It's like the universe whispers, "Let's make this happen for you!" This isn't about just taking; it's about understanding and flowing with the universe's natural energy. It's about filling yourself with appreciation and love, letting the universe write the most beautiful song for your life.

Writing a thank you letter to the universe is more than words on a page. It's about trusting, it's your heart talking to something so much bigger than you. It's knowing that the universe, in all its wonder, has a place for you, and it listens when you call out to it with a true heart. By doing this, you open the door to endless possibilities, building a life that feels amazing and true to you.

Steps to Writing Your Letter

Find Your Quiet Spot: Pick a peaceful place with no distractions so you can focus on your thoughts and feelings. The calmer you are, the deeper you can connect with yourself and what you want to say.

Why Are You Writing: Think about why you want to write this letter. What are you especially thankful for? Knowing this helps you write a heartfelt letter that shows the universe exactly how grateful you are.

Thank You from the Bottom of Your Heart: Right from the start, tell the universe how thankful you are. Mention specific things you appreciate, like supportive friends, your achievements, or even the little things that make you smile. Explain how these things make you feel – happy, proud, loved. The more you feel it, the clearer your message will be.

Be Specific and Feel It: Write about the things you're grateful for in detail, like painting a picture with words. As you write, remember how those moments made you feel, and let those feelings flow through your words. The more details you give and the deeper you feel, the stronger your connection to your gratitude becomes.

Big Thanks at the End: End your letter with a huge thank you to the universe for all the gifts, chances, and good things in your life. This last part shows the universe how much you mean it and makes your message even stronger.

Reflecting on Your Connection: Once you're done writing, you can fold the letter gently, like a secret you trust the universe with. You can also keep it somewhere special to make your gratitude practice even stronger. Re-reading your letter later can remind you of the power of gratitude and how it affects your life.

Writing to the universe isn't just a chore, it's a journey that changes you. As you do this more, you'll feel a closer connection to the universe. And the more you do it, the more the universe will answer your questions and bring you the things you desire. Try it for 21 days and see how it changes your life for the better. Embrace this journey, and let gratitude be your guiding light to a happier and more meaningful life.

"Write your wishes in the language of gratitude; the Universe understands and grants abundantly."

About the Author

Shivam Singh Bhadauriya

A visionary entrepreneur, soulful guide, and storyteller.

Entrepreneur

Shivam has been an entrepreneur since 2020. He co-founded Editvo Complete Advertising Solution, a Delhi-based digital marketing agency empowering businesses worldwide through exceptional marketing and advertising solutions.

Spiritual Coach

A professional spiritual coach, Shivam provides personalized guidance and support to individuals and entrepreneurs on their personal growth and development.

Content Creator

Shivam inspires and educates audiences on Instagram and YouTube with engaging and informative content.

Author

Shivam Singh Bhadauriya's debut book, The Heart Full of Thanks, offers profound insights into gratitude and personal transformation. You can buy the book on Amazon and Flipkart. If you want to learn more about the power of gratitude and how it can transform your life, The Heart Full of Thanks is the perfect guide.

www.ingramcontent.com/pod-product-compliance
Lightning Source LLC
LaVergne TN
LVHW050337160826
845677LV00014B/3654

* 9 7 8 9 3 6 0 8 1 9 3 9 2 *